Here is the wonderful and true story of Jesus, whom we call Jesus the Christ.
You can read more about him in the Bible.

A girl named Mary lived in the village of Nazareth in the district of Galilee a very long time ago.

She was engaged to marry Joseph, a carpenter, who was of the family of King David.

Before they were married, an astonishing thing happened: the angel Gabriel came to Mary and said, "Mary, God is very pleased with you. He's going to give you a baby son. Name the child Jesus. He will be a king whose kingdom will never end."

Some time later, Joseph went to Bethlehem to be taxed. He took Mary with him. While they were there, the baby, Jesus, was born.

In the fields around Bethlehem, shepherds were tending their sheep. That night the angel of the Lord came to tell them the good news about the baby.

"A Saviour, Christ the Lord, was born in Bethlehem today," the angel said.

The joyful shepherds hurried into Bethlehem and found Mary and Joseph, and the little Jesus lying in a manger.

The book of Matthew says
that wise men came
from the East to Jerusalem.
There they visited Herod,
King of the Jews.

"We're looking for the baby who will be King of the Jews,"
they said. "We saw his star in the east, and we want to
worship him."

"Oh no!" King Herod thought.
"That little boy might take my place!"

Out loud he said to the wise men,
"Well now, tell me when you find this child.
I'd like to worship him myself."

But he really intended to kill the baby.

The wise men followed the star to where Jesus was. They gave him wonderful gifts — gold and frankincense and myrrh. But they never went back to King Herod, because God told them not to.

An angel told Joseph that Herod wanted to kill Jesus. So Joseph took his little family to Egypt. They stayed there until it was safe for them to go home to Nazareth.

Jesus grew bigger and stronger and wiser.
Like other children, he played with his brothers and sisters and friends. He loved Mary and Joseph.
But he always knew that God was truly his Father.

Every spring Mary and Joseph went to Jerusalem for the Passover feast.
The year Jesus was twelve, he went with them.
When they were on their way home, Jesus couldn't be found.

The narrow road was crowded with people —
some walking, some riding donkeys.
"Maybe Jesus ran ahead with his cousins," Mary said.
"Maybe he lagged behind with some friends," said Joseph.

But when night fell and they hadn't found him yet,
they were upset.
"Let's go back to Jerusalem," Mary said.
"Perhaps he's still there."

All along the dusty road they looked for Jesus. But it was three days before they found him.
He was sitting among the teachers in the great temple, listening to them, and asking them questions.

"Oh Son!" Mary cried. "Your father and I have been so worried. Whatever made you stay here?"
Jesus looked up at them in surprise. "How could you worry?" he asked. "Don't you know I have to be about
my Father's business?" Mary and Joseph didn't understand what he meant. But Mary remembered what he said.
And Jesus never forgot that God was truly his Father.

Jesus became a carpenter like Joseph.

But he understood that his real work was to teach people about God, and to show them God's wonderful works.
So he went into all the towns and villages of Galilee, teaching in the synagogues and by the roadside.

He told everyone the good news that the kingdom of heaven is right here, right now.
He healed every kind of sickness
and every kind of trouble.

Once Jesus went up on a hillside with his disciples. He talked to them a long time about how to be close to God. People called that talk the Sermon on the Mount.

In it he told them how to obey God and what blessings are promised when we obey God.

We call these promises the Beatitudes.

He also talked about how to pray, and he gave the people the prayer that Christian people still pray today. It begins, "Our Father which art in heaven." We call it the Lord's Prayer.

He said, "Always treat other people the way you want them to treat you." We call this the Golden Rule.

You can read the Sermon on the Mount in the book of Matthew (Matt. 5—7). The book of Luke tells the Beatitudes, too. (Luke 6:20-23).

When Jesus talked to crowds, he sometimes spoke in parables.
A parable is a story that teaches a lesson.
It was as though Jesus was saying, "Now what I'm really telling you is like this. . . ."

Once a lot of bullies and troublemakers crowded around to hear him. Some Pharisees and scribes were there.
They didn't like what Jesus taught about God,
and they tried to make him seem bad.
"This fellow Jesus is pretty chummy with sinners,"
they muttered.

Jesus replied, "When you think about sinners, think about this:

If you had a hundred sheep and you lost one, wouldn't you leave the ninety-nine and hunt for that one lost sheep until you found it? Wouldn't you be glad and excited? You'd probably carry it straight home on your shoulders, and call all your friends and neighbors.
'Look!' you'd say. 'I found my lost sheep. Isn't that great?'"

"Well, that's the way it is about the kingdom of heaven and sinners," Jesus said. "There's more gladness in heaven over one sinner who's sorry and stops doing wrong than over ninety-nine people who never did anything wrong at all."

"What's the kingdom of heaven like?" someone asked.

"It's like the little mustard seed," Jesus answered. "When a man planted this tiny seed in his garden, it grew to be a bush so big that birds could perch in its branches."

Sometimes people listened to Jesus, but they didn't do what he told them to do.

"When you don't do what I tell you," Jesus said, "you're like a foolish man who built his house on sand. Pouring rain beat down on that house. Howling winds blew against it. And it fell with a mighty crash because it was built on sand."

"When you do what I tell you," he said, "you're like a wise man who built his house on a great strong rock. Pouring rain beat down on that house. Howling winds blew against it. But it didn't fall because it was built on a great strong rock."

Jesus told many parables like these to teach people about God and heaven and man.

Jesus could heal all kinds of trouble because he knew that God was truly his Father, and he trusted Him.

Great crowds followed Jesus everywhere.
They brought him friends and relatives who needed healing, and he healed them.

Bartimæus, a blind beggar, sat by the side of the road one day. When he heard that Jesus was close by, he shouted, "Jesus, Son of David, have mercy on me!"
"Oh, keep quiet!" some of the people snarled.
But Bartimæus shouted all the louder, "Son of David, have mercy on me!"

Jesus said, "Bring him to me."
Bartimæus jumped up, and came to Jesus.
"What do you want?" Jesus asked him.
"Master," blind Bartimæus said, "I want to be able to see."
"Your faith has ended your blindness," Jesus told him.
"You can be on your way right now, perfectly all right."

That very moment Bartimæus could see,
and he followed Jesus.

Another time, Jairus, the leader of the synagogue, fell on his knees before Jesus. "Please come home with me," he begged. "My little daughter is dying."
Before Jesus reached Jairus' house, a man rushed up from the leader's house. "Don't bother the Master," he said. "Your daughter's dead."
But Jesus told Jairus, "Don't be afraid. Just believe, and your little girl will be all right."

He and a few friends went to the house where everyone was crying. "Don't cry," Jesus said. "She isn't dead, she's sleeping."
"Sleeping!" they snorted. "That's all you know. She's dead."

But Jesus put everyone out of the little girl's room except her mother and father and his friends.
Then he took her by the hand and said, "Child, get up."
She got right up, and she was well.

Wouldn't you think everyone would be happy about healings like these? Well, they weren't. Some of the scribes and Pharisees weren't a bit happy. They tried to make it seem as if Jesus were doing something wrong — especially when he healed anyone on the Sabbath.

Once when he was teaching in a synagogue on the Sabbath, he saw a woman who couldn't stand up straight. She'd been that way for eighteen years.

"Woman," Jesus said, "you are now free." He laid his hands on her, and that very minute she stood up straight and began praising God.

The leader of this synagogue was furious. "There are six working days," he sputtered. "Anybody can come to be healed on one of them. Don't come on the Sabbath!"

"Wait a minute," Jesus answered. "Doesn't everyone take his ox or his donkey out of its stall on the Sabbath and lead it away to water? Isn't this woman as important as an ox or a donkey? Why shouldn't she be freed on the Sabbath from what was binding her?"

Most of the people in that synagogue agreed with Jesus. But others hated him more than ever.
Because Jesus proved what he said by healing whole crowds, more and more folks listened to him. Some of the Pharisees were afraid he was becoming more important than they were.
"This fellow is dangerous to us," they said. "He heals on the Sabbath. We think that's breaking the law."
"My Father never stops working," Jesus told them.
"And I must do whatever my Father does."
"Listen to him!" these Pharisees howled. "He thinks he's as good as God. Let's get rid of him!"

When Jesus first began teaching and healing, he chose twelve men to be his disciples — his special pupils.
He showed them how to heal the way he did.

They were Peter and his brother Andrew, James and his brother John, another James and his brother Judas, Philip, Bartholomew, Thomas, Matthew, Simon, and Judas Iscariot.

Jesus loved them all, and they loved him, too.
But one turned against him.

One day these Pharisees and a lot of their friends met at the temple with the high priest to decide how they should get rid of Jesus. While they were talking, Judas Iscariot came in. "What will you give me if I help you do away with Jesus?" he asked.

"Thirty pieces of silver," they answered.

As soon as he could, Judas Iscariot led the chief priests and elders and officers of the temple police to Jesus, and they captured him.

The next morning they took him straight to Pontius Pilate, the Roman governor. "Crucify him!" the crowds shouted. "We want him killed."

"Why?" the governor asked. "What wrong has he done?" But the crowds sent by the chief priests, lawyers, and elders, just kept shouting, "Crucify him! Crucify him!"

Finally the governor let them take Jesus,
and he was crucified. They nailed his hands
and his feet to a big wooden cross.

Jesus said, "Father, forgive them;
for they know not what they do."

The crowd booed and snickered and called out, "If you're
really the Son of God, come down from the cross.
You saved others — can't you save yourself?"

About three o'clock in the afternoon the soldiers saw
that he was dead.

The soldier standing guard nearby said, "Truly this man was the Son of God."

Joseph, a good man from Arimathea, asked the governor for Jesus' body. He took it down from the cross, wrapped it in linen cloth, and laid it in a cave hollowed out of rock. Joseph rolled a big stone against the opening of the cave to keep Jesus' body safe.

Very early on the first day of the week Mary Magdalene, whom Jesus had healed, came to the cave.
The big stone was rolled away!

Mary ran to tell the disciples. They didn't believe her, but Peter and another disciple went back with her.
They peered into the cave and saw the linen wrappings, but Jesus' body was gone.

The two disciples left Mary Magdalene standing outside the cave crying. Suddenly she looked up and saw Jesus, but she didn't recognize him.

"Why are you crying?" he asked.
"If you took Jesus' body, please tell me where it is," she said.

Jesus said, "Mary."
And right then she knew him.

"Tell my friends I'll meet them in Galilee," Jesus said.

No one believed her when Mary Magdalene said she had seen Jesus alive. And when two of his disciples saw him, no one believed them.

But before long all his closest disciples saw him. They ate with him, touched him, and talked with him.

"Go into all the world," he told them. "Tell everyone the good news about God and His love for man."
During the forty days after he came out of the cave alive, more than five hundred people saw Jesus.

Then, the Bible tells us, while he was talking with his disciples at the Mount of Olives, he lifted up his hands and blessed them. At that very moment he arose out of their sight. And they didn't see him again.

The people who hated Jesus and killed him for what he said and what he did, thought everyone would soon forget him. Instead of that, what he said and what he did are still being talked about — more than two thousand years later.
So today what Jesus said and what he did are helping people everywhere in the world.

Dear Parent,

The Story of Jesus offers important lessons about his life and works. Beginning with the nativity, it highlights the significant aspects of Christ Jesus' life in a way that will delight and inspire children and adults alike.

Children will quickly see through the sly cunning of Herod when he asked about the baby Jesus. They will travel with the twelve-year-old Jesus to the Passover feast in Jerusalem and realize, as his mother did, the significance of Jesus' understanding that he was about his "Father's business." The book tells, simply and directly, his teachings, stories, and healings. Throughout the story, children will discover the love and concern Jesus had for them as expressed in his words: "Suffer little children, and forbid them not, to come unto me: for of such is the kingdom of heaven" (Matthew 19:14). "Jesus loved little children," as Mary Baker Eddy, the Discoverer and Founder of Christian Science, points out, "because of their freedom from wrong and their receptiveness of right" (*Science and Health with Key to the Scriptures*, p. 236).

Skillfully told by Jean Horton Berg, an experienced storyteller and children's book author, *The Story of Jesus* will inspire new insights and learning about Jesus' remarkable life in children of all ages.

The Story of Jesus — A Bible story for children imaginatively retold and adapted by Jean Horton Berg from the books of the Gospels in the King James Version

Illustrated by Beth and Joe Krush

THE CHRISTIAN SCIENCE PUBLISHING SOCIETY
Boston, Massachusetts, USA

G50745

ISBN 978-0-87510-460-7